Y0-AGK-884

CRAZY CREATURES
Balloon Modeling

Written by the Top That! team

TOPTHAT!Kids™

Copyright © 2003 Top That Publishing plc,
Top That! USA, 27023 McBean Parkway, #408 Valencia, CA 91355
Top That! is a Registered Trademark of Top That! Publishing plc
www.topthatpublishing.com

PRACTICAL TIPS

Balloon animals are easy and great fun to make. Here are some basic tips to get you started.

What kind of balloons?

The models in this book use balloons 12 inches long. Fully inflated, they could be five times this size.

How much air?

Balloons are easiest to work if they are only half-full of air. If you fill them with too much air, they might burst. Follow the instructions for each model carefully.

How should I inflate the balloons?

Use a balloon pump. Pump until your balloon reaches the length you need. Remove the pump, then tie a knot in the end of the balloon.

How important are measurements?

Measurements given for bubble lengths are just a guide to help you start. Once you get the hang of them, you can develop the models in any way you want!

DO THE TWIST!

All balloon animals are made from sausage-shaped bubbles: pinched, twisted, and held together by the stretch of the balloon and the tension between the bubbles. Magic!

Lock twist

A twist is two full turns of the balloon, making a bubble. Twist two bubbles together at the joint to 'lock' them in place.

Ear twist

The second bubble is bent over and double-twisted at the point where it joins the first.

Always ask an adult to help you as some of the twists and turns are quite tricky!

3

PRACTICE
MAKES
PERFECT

Take time to practice these basic steps before you start on a model. For each model you make, choose your favorite color from the balloons in this pack.

1 Use a balloon blown up to 18 inches. Hold the balloon with your left hand at the knotted end. Pinch the balloon about 14 inches from the knot with your first finger and thumb.

2 Twist the rest of the balloon twice with your right hand. Hold the twist tightly.

3 Slide your right hand along the balloon a further 4 inches. Make a pinch and double twist.

4 Fold the balloon over at this second twist. Hold it in place with your left thumb and finger.

5 Slide your right hand along the balloon and pinch another 4 inch bubble. Make another double twist.

6 Hold the first twist and the last twist together firmly with your left hand. Twist the two middle bubbles twice to lock them together.

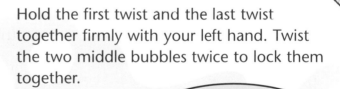

Practice drawing features onto your animals. Use a marker pen or permanent felt-tips. Be careful not to get any ink on your clothes or your surroundings!

DOG

You will need only one balloon to make this cute little dog.

1 Inflate a balloon to 24 inches. Make two 3 ½ inch bubbles at the knotted end of the balloon. Fold the second bubble over and ear twist it to make a nose and ears.

2 Make three 3 inch bubbles along the balloon. Lock the first and third twists to make a neck and two front legs.

6

3 Make three more bubbles: one 4 inch and two 3 inch. Lock the first and third twists together. Turn the back legs so that they line up with the front ones.

The remaining part of the balloon will form the tail. Finally, draw on all the features and add the sticker eyes to complete your model.

LITTLE LADYBUG

Create this lovely ladybug in four easy steps.

1. Inflate a red balloon to 10 inches and tie a knot in the end. For the head, twist a 1 ¹/₂ inch bubble and wrap the knot of the balloon into the twist to secure the bubble, as shown in B.

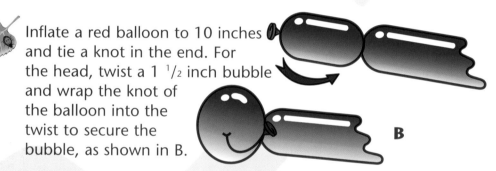

B

2. Now twist six 1 inch bubbles to form the ladybug's legs. Lock twist bubbles A and B at the base of the head.

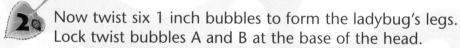

A   B

3 Now twist a 2 ½ inch bubble. Hold the twist securely and ask an adult to deflate the rest of the balloon by snipping the far end with scissors.

4 Tie off the balloon at the last twist and cut off the deflated section. Wrap the knot between the two back legs to secure. This bubble is the ladybug's body.

Add cute little features to the ladybug's face.

DON'T FORGET THE SPOTS ON HER BACK!

GIRAFFE

When making this gentle giant, take care when working the small bubbles for its ears; squeeze out some air if necessary.

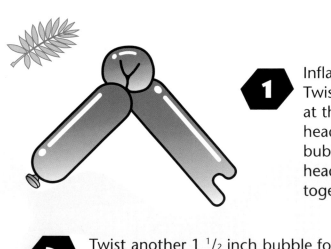

1 Inflate a balloon to 30 inches. Twist a single 3 $1/2$ inch bubble at the knotted end for the head. Now twist a 1 $1/2$ inch bubble. Fold it back to the head and ear twist the two together.

2 Twist another 1 $1/2$ inch bubble for the second ear. Bend this back in the same way as the first and ear twist it in place behind the head.

10

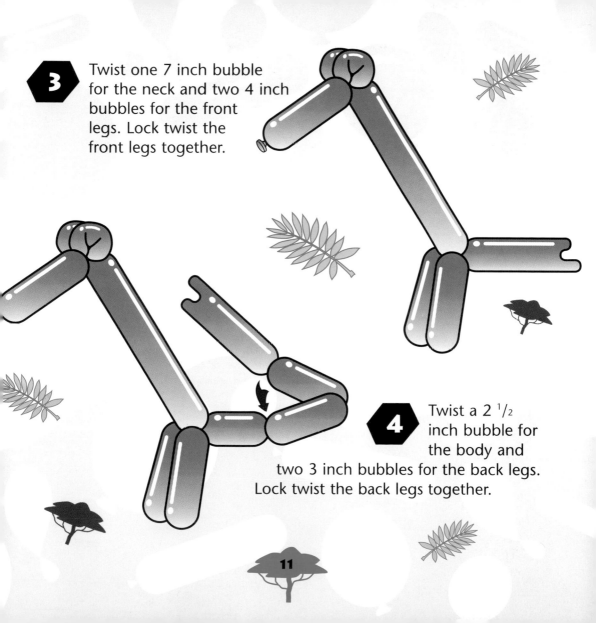

3 Twist one 7 inch bubble for the neck and two 4 inch bubbles for the front legs. Lock twist the front legs together.

4 Twist a 2 ½ inch bubble for the body and two 3 inch bubbles for the back legs. Lock twist the back legs together.

11

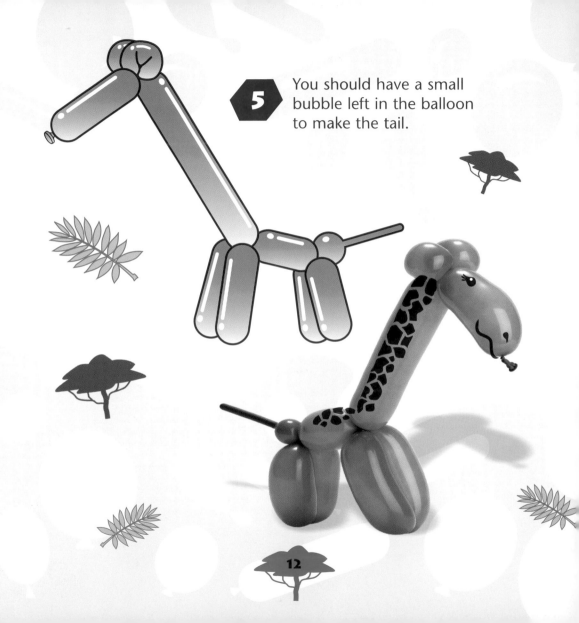

You should have a small
bubble left in the balloon
to make the tail.

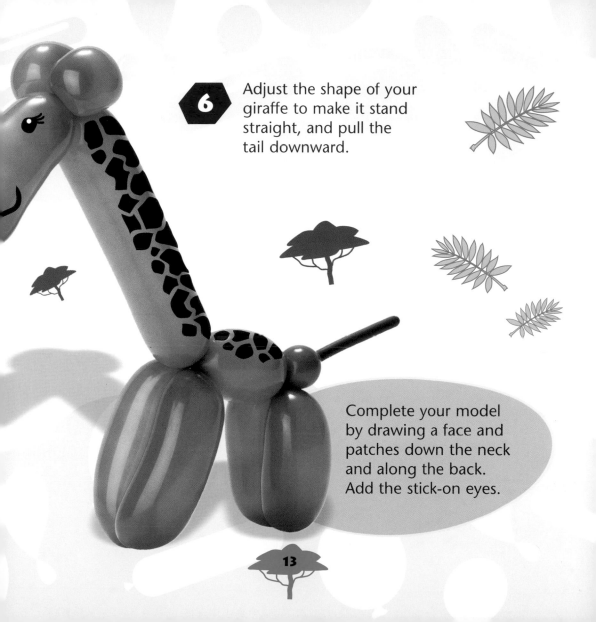

6 Adjust the shape of your giraffe to make it stand straight, and pull the tail downward.

Complete your model by drawing a face and patches down the neck and along the back. Add the stick-on eyes.

13

CHUNKY THE CATERPILLAR

Chunky the caterpillar is quite tricky to make—ask an adult to help you.

1 Inflate a balloon, leaving a 2 inch tip uninflated, and tie a knot in the end. Twist a 1 inch bubble and ear twist it to make a bug head, tucking in the knot to secure it.

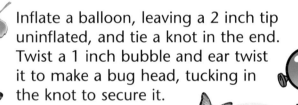

2 Now twist a 9 ½ inch bubble. Fold it in half and lock twist it.

14

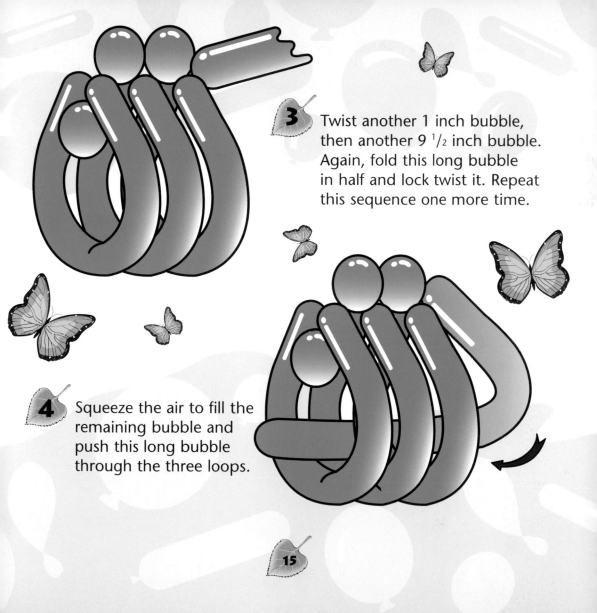

3 Twist another 1 inch bubble, then another 9 ½ inch bubble. Again, fold this long bubble in half and lock twist it. Repeat this sequence one more time.

4 Squeeze the air to fill the remaining bubble and push this long bubble through the three loops.

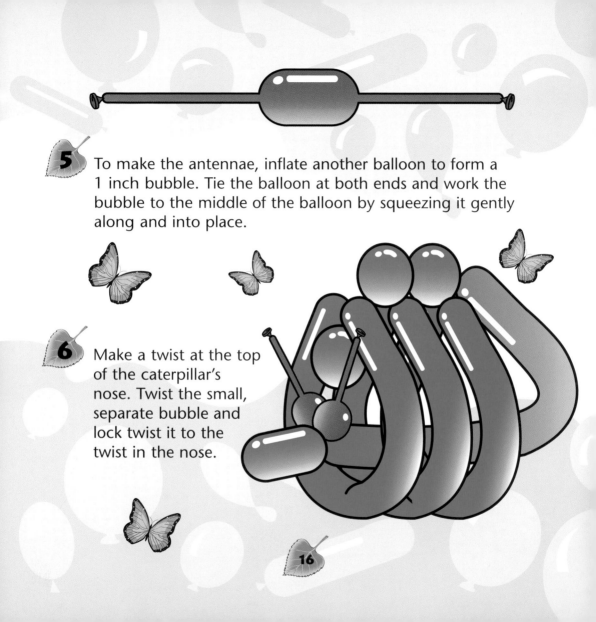

5 To make the antennae, inflate another balloon to form a 1 inch bubble. Tie the balloon at both ends and work the bubble to the middle of the balloon by squeezing it gently along and into place.

6 Make a twist at the top of the caterpillar's nose. Twist the small, separate bubble and lock twist it to the twist in the nose.

16

RHINOCEROS

Unlike the previous models, this one is started tail first!

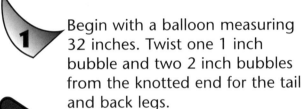

1 Begin with a balloon measuring 32 inches. Twist one 1 inch bubble and two 2 inch bubbles from the knotted end for the tail and back legs.

2 Fold the second leg over the first and lock twist them together to the tail.

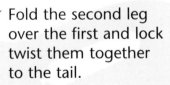

18

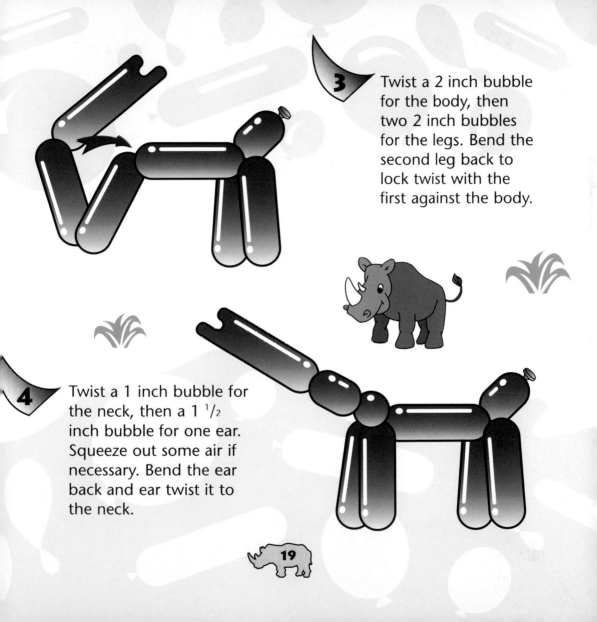

3 Twist a 2 inch bubble for the body, then two 2 inch bubbles for the legs. Bend the second leg back to lock twist with the first against the body.

4 Twist a 1 inch bubble for the neck, then a 1 ¹/₂ inch bubble for one ear. Squeeze out some air if necessary. Bend the ear back and ear twist it to the neck.

19

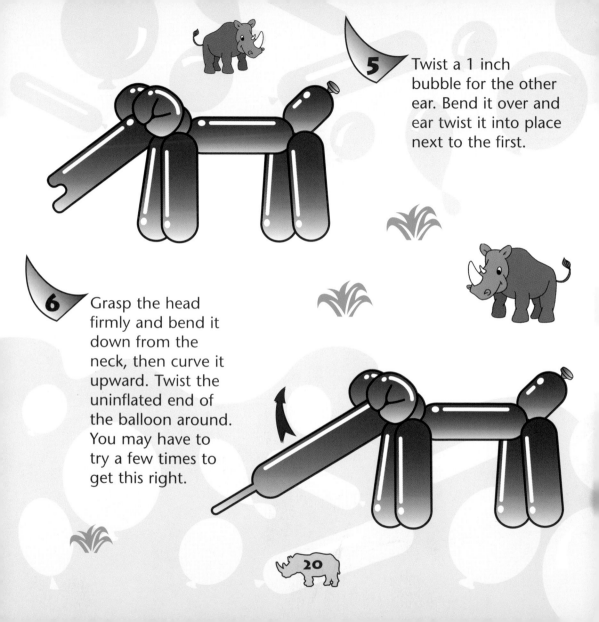

Twist a 1 inch bubble for the other ear. Bend it over and ear twist it into place next to the first.

6 Grasp the head firmly and bend it down from the neck, then curve it upward. Twist the uninflated end of the balloon around. You may have to try a few times to get this right.

20

You should have about 4 inches of balloon left to make the head.

Finish off your rhinoceros by drawing eyes and a mouth with a permanent felt-tip pen.

21

SWAN

This model uses two balloons. Use white for a mute swan or black for a more exotic variety.

1 Blow up the first balloon to the end (remembering not to over-inflate it). Tie the ends together to form a loop.

2 Twist the loop into a figure eight, keeping the knot at one end. You should now have two rings: one plain and one with a knot.

22

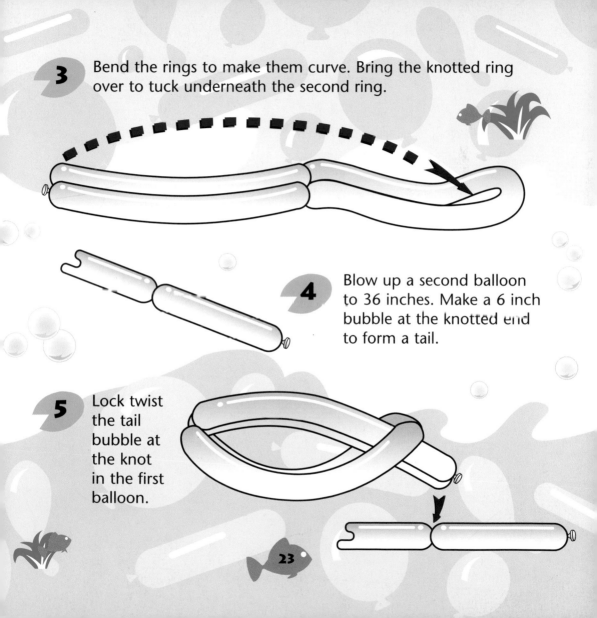

3 Bend the rings to make them curve. Bring the knotted ring over to tuck underneath the second ring.

4 Blow up a second balloon to 36 inches. Make a 6 inch bubble at the knotted end to form a tail.

5 Lock twist the tail bubble at the knot in the first balloon.

23

6 Twist an 8 inch bubble in the second balloon to make the body. Lock twist it to the joint of the two rings in the first balloon. The remaining bubble will form the swan's neck and head.

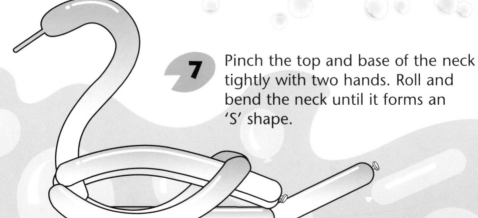

7 Pinch the top and base of the neck tightly with two hands. Roll and bend the neck until it forms an 'S' shape.

Complete your model with features and eyes drawn with a permanent felt-tip or marker.

MOUSE

Some very small bubbles make up this little character. Once again, you will need to squeeze the air out of some of them before you twist, so that they are only half as fat as the main balloon.

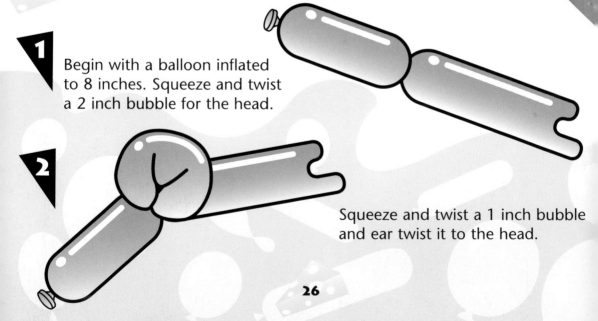

1 Begin with a balloon inflated to 8 inches. Squeeze and twist a 2 inch bubble for the head.

2

Squeeze and twist a 1 inch bubble and ear twist it to the head.

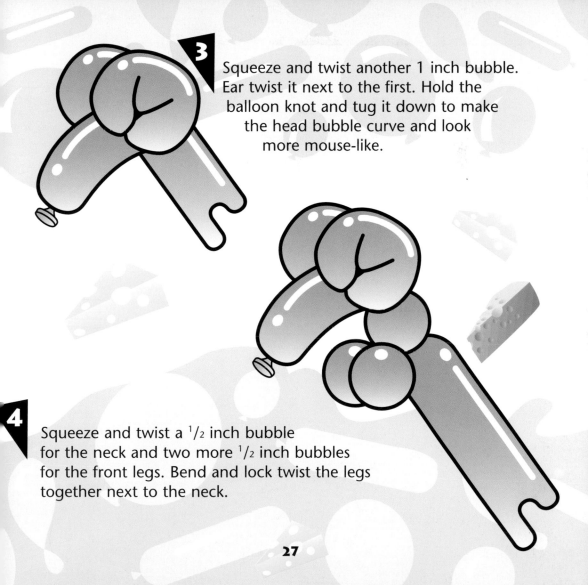

3

Squeeze and twist another 1 inch bubble. Ear twist it next to the first. Hold the balloon knot and tug it down to make the head bubble curve and look more mouse-like.

Squeeze and twist a $1/2$ inch bubble for the neck and two more $1/2$ inch bubbles for the front legs. Bend and lock twist the legs together next to the neck.

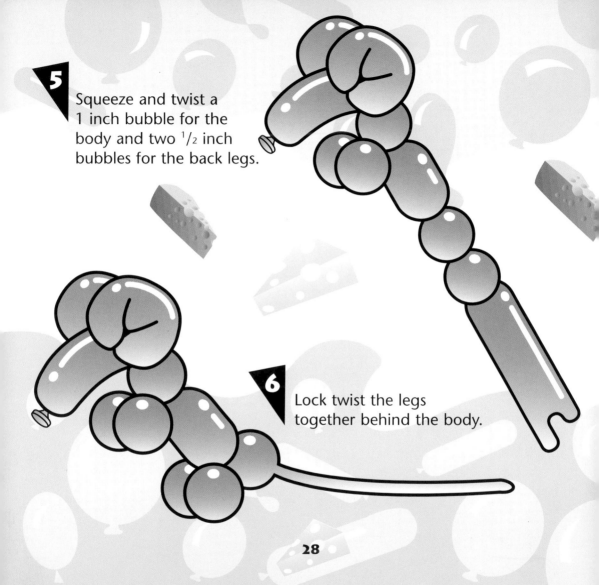

5 Squeeze and twist a 1 inch bubble for the body and two 1/2 inch bubbles for the back legs.

6 Lock twist the legs together behind the body.

28

You should have a small bubble
($^1/_2$ inch) and a long piece of balloon
left over for the mouse's tail.
Finish your mouse by drawing
eyes, a nose, and whiskers
with a felt-tip pen.

KANGAROO

Red, brown, or gray are good colors for this kangaroo. Squeeze some air from the smaller bubbles to make them easier to work with.

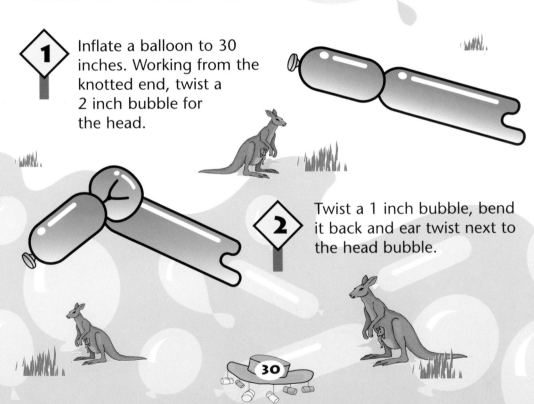

1 Inflate a balloon to 30 inches. Working from the knotted end, twist a 2 inch bubble for the head.

2 Twist a 1 inch bubble, bend it back and ear twist next to the head bubble.

30

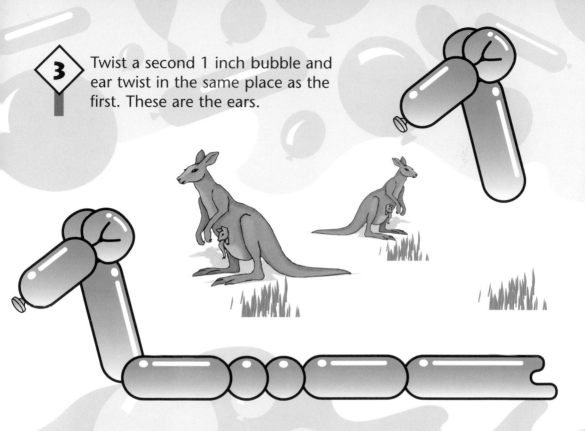

3 Twist a second 1 inch bubble and ear twist in the same place as the first. These are the ears.

4 Now, twist a 3 inch bubble for the neck, a 2 ½ inch bubble, two 1 inch bubbles, and another 2 ½ inch bubble. These will form the neck, front legs, and paws.

31

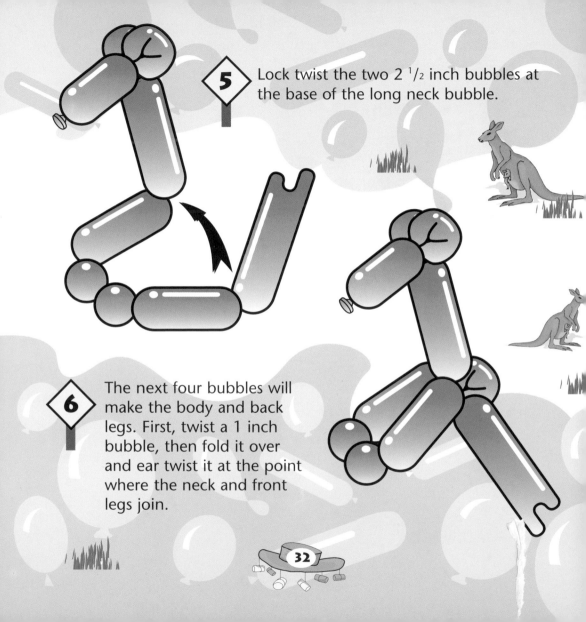

5 Lock twist the two 2 ¹/₂ inch bubbles at the base of the long neck bubble.

6 The next four bubbles will make the body and back legs. First, twist a 1 inch bubble, then fold it over and ear twist it at the point where the neck and front legs join.

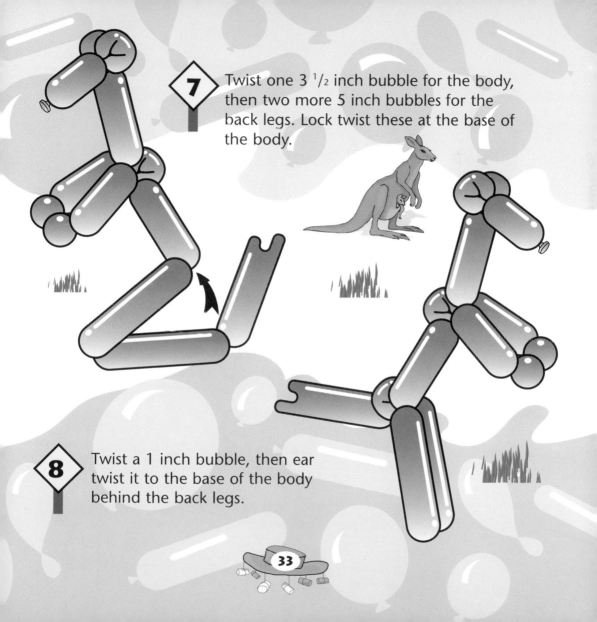

7 Twist one 3 ¹/₂ inch bubble for the body, then two more 5 inch bubbles for the back legs. Lock twist these at the base of the body.

8 Twist a 1 inch bubble, then ear twist it to the base of the body behind the back legs.

9 Squeeze the air gently along the remaining balloon to make the kangaroo's tail, curving it upward as you press. Gently curve and shape the kangaroo body, legs and tail so that it stands upright.

34

Complete your model with eyes
and a smiling mouth, drawn with
a permanent felt-tip or marker.
Finish with the stick-on eyes.

HUMMINGBIRD

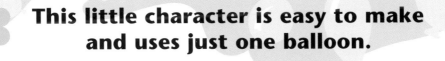

This little character is easy to make and uses just one balloon.

1 Inflate a balloon to 32 inches. Twist one 2 inch bubble at the knotted end for the body, then one 2 ¹/₂ inch bubble at the other end for the head. The long piece of uninflated balloon will form the beak.

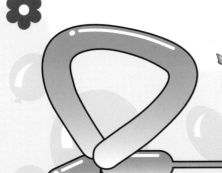

2 Bend the middle bubble over and lock twist the head and tail together. This should give you a large loop.

3 Pinch the centre of the loop, press down, and lock twist it to the neck to form the wings.

Finish your model with a face and some feathers on its back. For a more exotic look, use glitter to decorate the wings.

CRAZY CENTIPEDE

This model looks best if you use balloons in the same color.

 1 Inflate two balloons to half their length and tie off. Twist a 2 inch bubble in the first balloon and make a bug head.

 2 Now twist a 1 inch bubble for the neck, then two more 1 inch bubbles. Ear twist both of these to form legs.

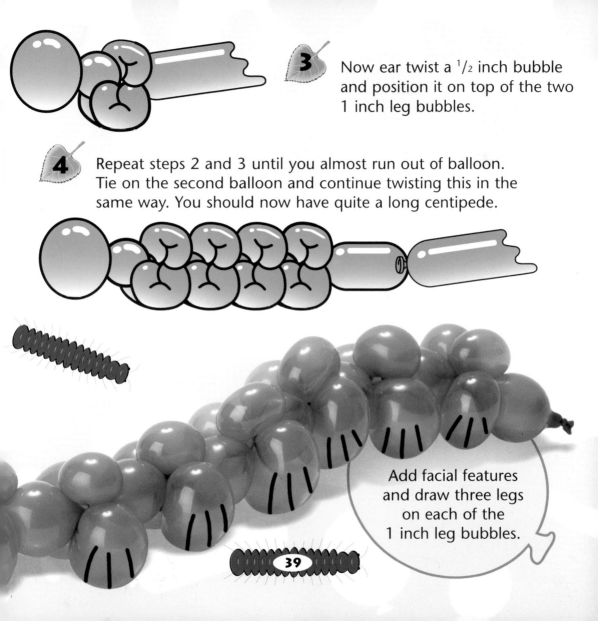

3 Now ear twist a $^1/_2$ inch bubble and position it on top of the two 1 inch leg bubbles.

4 Repeat steps 2 and 3 until you almost run out of balloon. Tie on the second balloon and continue twisting this in the same way. You should now have quite a long centipede.

Add facial features and draw three legs on each of the 1 inch leg bubbles.

CROCODILE

To make this snappy chap, squeeze some air out of the smaller bubbles before you twist (this makes it easier to work). They need half the amount of air of the larger bubbles.

1 Blow up a balloon to 14 inches. Twist a 4 inch bubble from the knotted end for the face. Squeeze and twist a 2 inch bubble for one eye. Bend the eye bubble back and ear twist it to the head. Ear twist another 2 inch bubble for the second eye.

2 Squeeze and twist a 1 inch bubble for the neck. Twist a 6 inch bubble for the first leg. Bend this bubble over and ear twist it behind the neck.

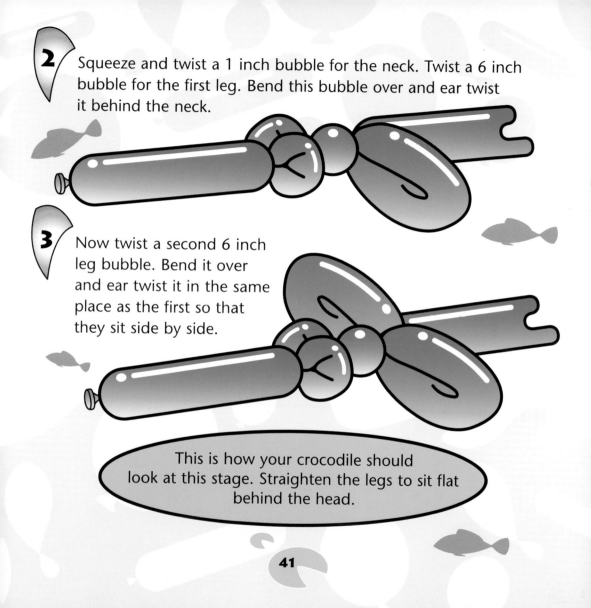

3 Now twist a second 6 inch leg bubble. Bend it over and ear twist it in the same place as the first so that they sit side by side.

This is how your crocodile should look at this stage. Straighten the legs to sit flat behind the head.

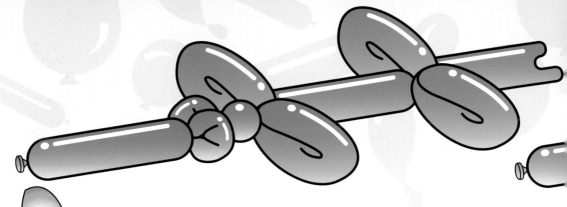

4 Twist a 4 ¹/₂ inch bubble for the body and a 6 inch bubble for a back leg. Bend this over and ear twist it behind the body. Make another 6 inch bubble and ear twist it to make the second leg. Straighten the legs to lie flat.

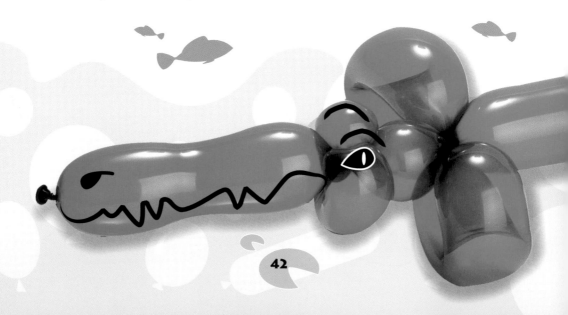

5 You'll have a small bubble left over. Squeeze the air along the remaining piece of balloon to make the croc's tail.

Finish the crocodile with a drawn-on face (and the stick-on eyes) and scales drawn along the tail.

PARROT & SWING

This model calls for brightly-colored balloons and string or ribbon to hang the swing. Don't forget to squeeze some air out of the small bubbles.

Inflate a 24 inch balloon and twist a 1 inch bubble.

Twist a 2 inch bubble. Lock twist the knot around this second bubble. Tuck it between the two bubbles and hold it tight.

44

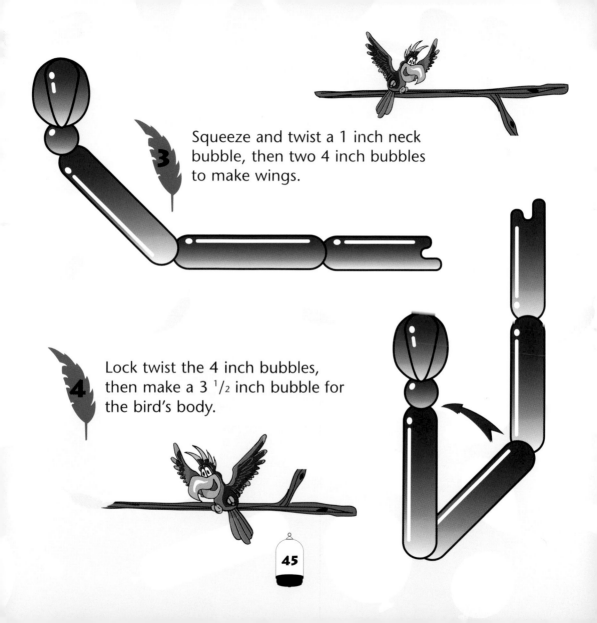

Squeeze and twist a 1 inch neck bubble, then two 4 inch bubbles to make wings.

3

Lock twist the 4 inch bubbles, then make a 3 1/2 inch bubble for the bird's body.

4

45

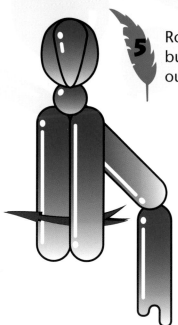

5 Roll the 3 1/2 inch bubble between the two wing bubbles. Adjust it to form the bird's puffed out chest.

6 Now twist two 1 1/2 inch bubbles, bending and ear twisting them to the body to form the feet.

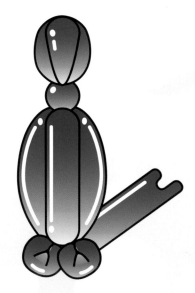

7 Gently squeeze the air along the remaining section of balloon to make a tapering tail.

Finish your parrot with stick-on eyes and claws drawn with a felt-tip pen. Turn the page to see how to make his swing.

TO MAKE THE PARROT'S SWING

1 Inflate a balloon almost to the end. Measure 6 inches from the knot then ear twist a 1 inch bubble.

2 Ear twist a second 1 inch bubble from the other end. Bring this bubble around to lock twist with the knot of the balloon.

Adjust the shape, so that it hangs straight, and put your parrot in the middle of the crossbar. Tie a ribbon or string to the top and hang it somewhere where it can gently swing in the breeze.